GW01216543

Parenting with an Edge

A Pocket Guide to Raise
Strong & Confident Kids

Michele Sfakianos, RN, BSN

Open Pages Publishing, LLC
P.O. Box 61048
Fort Myers, FL 33906
http://www.my411books.com
(239) 454-7700

ISBN: (e) 978-0-9836-6466-6
ISBN: (sc) 978-0-9836-6467-3

Library of Congress Control Number: 2013941757

This book is dedicated to all parents who wish to raise strong, confident, and well-mannered children.

Acknowledgments

Thank you to everyone who has supported: "The 4-1-1 on Life Skills;" "The 4-1-1 on Step Parenting;" and "The 4-1-1 on Surviving Teenhood." I am fortunate to live my passion to help others.

Thank you to my family and friends for encouraging me to share this information with you.

Foreword

It all starts with a stick...those two minutes you have to wait are the longest two minutes of your life...then you get the "+" sign. You are pregnant! You will be someone's parent. You spend the next nine months preparing for your baby. You realize that there are so many things to do; so many things to buy; and so many things to learn. You also realize that children do not come with instruction manuals. Now what?

You can rely on books that your family and friends recommend or the internet. Your parents, and other caregivers you had, will give you some of the best advice, but take all of this with a grain of salt because no certain way is perfect and not every parenting tip works for everyone.

Once you learn you are pregnant your whole world and the way you see things change immediately. You will start seeing babies everywhere and begin making judgments of other parents.

You may see a sweet interaction between and mother and daughter and think I can't wait! Then you will see a negative interaction between a mother and daughter and think am I really ready for this?

Many adults struggle with raising children partly because of the importance of parental responsibility. As a parent, it is our responsibility to meet the needs of our children. You will be responsible for basic needs such as water; nutritious food; shelter; a warm bed with clean sheets, blanket and a pillow; medical care; clothing; and personal space. You will want to provide an environment that is safe. You will be responsible for providing their self-esteem needs and the morals and values of your family. As a parent, we want to develop a discipline system to create the mutual respect every family member deserves. These are the basics.

Aside from the basics, one of the most important things a parent can give their child is a sense of being loved. We must give unconditional love and support. Tell them that you love them every day. Tell them that there is nothing they could ever do or say that would cause you to stop loving them. Tell them that you are in their corner on every issue. Spend time with them. Show them that they are the priority in your life. Support their endeavors even if they choose a path that you would never choose or didn't want them to choose.

Table of Contents

Chapter One

What's Your Parenting Style?

"It's no use saying, "We are doing our best." You have got to succeed in doing what is necessary."
                                        -Winston Churchill

What a difficult life a child leads today. Are our children forced to live on the edge at a super-ficial level with no acceptance and minimal positive affirmation from parents? Is the peer pressure too much? Are they learning to live from the Internet and television with no emphasis on moral values or excellence? Are you comfortable with your parenting style? Or, do you need to tweak some things? Only you can answer these questions.

Raising children in today's world is a tough challenge. After all, kids don't come with an instruction manual. New parent's often feel helpless and you must take comfort in knowing that this is a natural, very normal, response.

Parenting Styles

A parenting style involves a child rearing behavior (of parents, guardians, or other primary caregivers) that involves the amount of control over a child's activities and behavior and the degree of nurturance of the child. Parents can create their own styles from a combination of factors, and these can change over time as the children develop their own personalities and move through life's stages. Is there one style that works best for all children? No. Parenting styles are affected by both the parents' and child's temperaments and is largely based on the influence of one's own parents and culture. Most people learn parenting practices from their own parents. These parents can decide to accept or discard those practices.

Types of parenting styles, a sample of the top five:

1. Authoritative: These parents demand and respond, as characterized by a child-centered

approach, and hold high expectations of maturity for the child. Typical traits of authoritative parents:

- Warm and responsive and strive toward meeting their children's physical and emotional needs.
- Provide rules and guidance without being overbearing.
- Offer relative freedom of choice by encouraging independent thinking and give-and-take discussions.
- Will forgive and teach, instead of punishing the child if he or she falls short.
- Were raised in a spirit of disciplined conformity, general obedience, and adherence to rules. Basically, the children do what they are told to do.
- Produce children who are more independent and self-reliant.

2. Indulgent or Permissive Parenting: These parents respond but do not demand. Also called lenient and are characterized as having few

behavioral expectations for the child. Typical traits of indulgent parents:

- Meet the child's needs and are warm, responsive, and caring.
- Do not require children to regulate themselves.
- Use a nonrestrictive child-discipline strategy.
- Tend to evade conflicts, embrace harmony, and encourage give-and-take discussions.
- Encourage independent thinking.

3. Christian Parenting: These parents use the application of Biblical principles on parenting. Some Christian parents follow a strict and more authoritarian interpretation of the Bible, and others are "grace-based" and share other methods. Typical traits of Christian parents:

- Teach their children about formalized religion and religious practices.
- Teach children to memorize and meditate on scripture.
- Nourish their children with wholesome discipline and encourage them to build a

personal relationship with God and to live a Christian life.

- Teach their children about forgiveness.
- Adhere to a clean life free of drugs, smoking, and other outside temptations.
- Encourage honesty and truthfulness.

4. Attachment Parenting or Natural Parenting: These parents seek to create a strong emotional bond and avoid physical punishment. Typical traits of attachment or natural parents:

- Seek to create a special bond.
- Respond with sensitivity.
- Practice positive discipline. Parents are encouraged to work out a solution together with a child, rather than spanking or simply imposing their will on the child.
- Strive for balance in personal and family life. Parents are encouraged to create a support network, live a healthy lifestyle, and prevent parenting burnout.

5. Helicopter Parenting: Helicopter parents keep their children at close range; always "hover-

ing" above them, trying to make sure no harm will come to them. Typical traits of helicopter parents:

- Helicopter parents don't believe their children can take care of themselves, and they fear that if they don't keep tight control over everything, harm will come to their children.
- Often over-program their children and fail to allow them free time to play and explore on their own.
- Well known in the school system.
- Will complete basic tasks for their children, such as: homework, job applications, and college applications.
- Will try to solve all of their problems and sweep all obstacles out of the way.

Other parenting styles:

- Authoritarian: Parents that demand but do not respond (Strict Parenting), characterized by high expectations on conformity and compliance to parental rules and directions, while allowing little open dialogue between parent and child.

- Positive Parenting: Positive parenting works to empower children.
- Conscious Parenting or Unconditional Parenting: These parents show unconditional love rather than conditionally. They are against positive reinforcement parenting, meaning if the child behaves, the parent will show him love, and if he doesn't, the parent will not show him love.
- Slow Parenting: This style encourages parents to plan and organize less for their children, instead allowing them to enjoy their childhood and explore the world at their own pace.
- Negligent or Uninvolved Parenting: Neglectful parenting neither demands nor responds, also called hands-off parenting. The parents are low in responsiveness and do not set limits.
- Nurturant Parenting: A family model where children are expected to explore

their surroundings with the protection of their parents.

- Narcissistic Parenting: These parents thirst for external recognition and acceptance and unconsciously use their children as a means to live out dreams and fantasies they never got to realize.
- Toxic Parenting: These parents range from children's needs to direct physical, emotional, and sometimes even sexual abuse.
- Shared Parenting: This style results when married parents equally share the responsibility of parenting and the responsibility of earning money.
- Punishment-based Parenting: These parents use pain, punishment, intimidation, yelling, degradation, humiliation, shame, guilt, or other things to hurt a child's self-esteem, or they hurt them physically. Punishment-based parenting also damages the relationship between the parent and child. It puts unnecessary pressure on the child, and the child is less apt to perform due to pressure.

No one parenting style is right or wrong. Parenting is a lifelong job of trials and errors, and hindsight is always 20/20. All parents must decide for themselves how to raise their children. There are no fixed rules, no written instructions, and no child manual. There are situations in all of our lives that influence the way we do things, both consciously and subconsciously. The way we were raised, and the time and place we were raised in, are all factors that play an important role in how we raise our children. Parents should keep an open mind to the choices other parents make, learning about the parenting styles of other cultures, and consider if there are things we should all do differently. No two kids are alike. What works for one child may not work for another. Find what works for your child.

Chapter Two

Positive Parenting Behaviors

"There should never be any yelling in the home unless there is a fire." -David O. McKay

Taking Action

As parents, guardians, or caregivers, we should all be taking the following actions:

- Be yourself.
- Love and respect yourself and others.
- Listen respectfully to one another.
- Build the lines of communication. Always communicate in a positive manner. Never give them an "I told you so" response. Let them know they can talk to you about anything.
- Keep an open and nonjudgmental atmosphere.
- Address conflict in a positive manner.
- Do things and go places together.

- Show affection to one another comfortably.
- Have respect for everyone's personal space.
- Be flexible.
- Shed anger and bitterness.
- Be honest.
- Be patient.
- Keep your sense of humor.
- Compromise.
- Be understanding.
- Show unconditional love.
- Remember to enjoy your kids.
- Assist your children with their homework, but don't DO the homework.
- Keep the spark in your marriage. Spend time together away from the children.
- Encourage a relationship between the children and their biological parent, not living with them, if in a "step" relationship.
- Include the children in the moving details, decorating and home needs.
- Explain to the children (if of age to understand), the financial situation of the family.

Positive Parenting Behaviors

- Establish core family values and live by them. Establish rules, set limits, and ensure conformity to those rules and limits.
- Make new memories in different ways.
- Be their parent, their moral compass, their guide, not their friend. Children emulate those they know best.
- Encourage your child to be an individual, not a follower, and encourage independence.
- Take responsibility for what you expose your small children and teens to daily. (TV, movies, video games)
- Monitor television, computers, cell phones, and other communication devices. Set and reinforce limits on your child's media use. Watch TV and movies together to better connect and discuss the messages sent about body image and other expectations.
- Provide a healthy and complete meal and sit down together as a family to enjoy it. Use mealtime to talk about things going on in each other's lives.

- Respect his or her opinion and take into account his or her thoughts and feelings. It's important your child knows you are listening.

- Engage in active listening. Active listening is a communication technique that requires the listener to understand, interpret, and evaluate what is heard. Once you hear your child's concerns, you will be able to feel what he or she feels. Active listening gives the child the opportunity to correct you. In other words: they talk, you listen, and you paraphrase what they said to you, and they tell you if you are correct. Doing so helps to fix any misunderstandings.

- Be honest and direct when talking about sensitive subjects such as sex, drugs, drinking, and smoking.

- Children want the chance to be trusted. Give them a chance.

- Be willing to admit you don't know everything and that you're not always right.

- Provide a supportive and encouraging environment. Focus on the positive, instead of criticizing, praise their special talents, and nurture their interests. Children want their parents to be proud of them.

- Children need their home to be a refuge, a safe haven.
- Model and teach positive stress management and coping skills. Children need help managing the stresses and pressure in their lives.
- Know your kid's friends.
- Never shame them when you find out something you don't approve of. Even "good" kids act out once in a while.
- Help your small children and teens build their self-esteem by teaching them techniques of goal achievement. Have them break down their big goals into small, achievable goals in order to alleviate some of the stress in their lives.
- Look out for signs of stress, anxiety, lack of concentration, poor food and drink intake, personal hygiene changes, sleep disturbances, lack of interest in social activities, and then address them immediately.

- Keep the medicine cabinet locked. Unlocked medicine cabinets are an open invitation for kids and their friends to abuse prescription drugs.
- Know that addiction runs in families and be proactive to prevent it.
- Know that addiction is a health problem and can be treated.
- Understand alcohol, tobacco, and substance abuse is preventable.
- Understand there's no shame in accepting professional help.

Chapter Three

Negative Parenting Behaviors

"Those who look for the bad in people will surely find it." -Abraham Lincoln

Don't Be a Negative Nellie!

We've discussed the things you should be doing. Below are the things you should NOT do:

- Argue with a child.
- Be intrusive (unless you think there is a problem which could escalate into a horrific event.)
- Judge.
- Criticize.
- React out of emotion.
- Force the new relationship, if in a "step" child situation.
- Choose sides.
- Be quick to jump to conclusions.
- Try to reason with an angry child.

- Give consequences or punishment in the heat of the moment.
- Make threats in the heat of the moment.
- Lose sight of your family goals and values.
- Miss out on important milestones in your child's life. (Recital, sporting game, awards presentation, etc.)
- Let the ex-partner be dependent on you.
- Keep the children from their biological parent (unless it is a court-order or in the best interest of the child.)
- Keep the children from their grandparents (both maternal and paternal).
- Fight with your partner, your ex-partner or their ex-partner in front of the children. Keep your differences behind closed doors.
- Cancel on visiting or spending time with your child.
- Bad mouth the ex-partner or their family members.
- Try and buy their love.
- Take things personal.
- If you are responsible to pay child support, do not withhold child support. The kids

should not be punished for things they
have no control.

Chapter Four

Positive Praise

"I'm a success today because I had a friend who believed in me and I didn't have the heart to let him down." –Abraham Lincoln

Don't Over-Praise Your Children

Parents everywhere praise their kids when they do well in school, sports, or anything that maybe didn't take a lot of effort to accomplish. Did you know that too much praise or putting a child on a pedestal at an early age can hinder their growth? By giving kids lots of praise, parents think they build their children's self-esteem and confidence, but it just may be doing the opposite. Too much praise, and at the wrong time, can backfire. It can cause children to be afraid to try new things or fear not being able to perform to their parent's expectations. In fact, kids who are told they're bright and talented are easily discouraged when something is "too diffi-cult;" those who are not praised in such a manner are more motivated to work harder and take on greater challenges. Those not praised, in turn, show higher levels of confidence, while over-praised are more likely to lie to make their per-formances sound better. Praise becomes like a drug: once they get it, they need it, want it, are unable to function without it. On the other hand, not giving enough praise can be just as damaging as giving too much.

While there's no secret formula for praise, ex-perts say understanding the where, when, and how of praising children is an important tool in raising confident kids with a high sense of self-esteem. The quality of praise is more important than the quantity. Your praise should be sincere and genuine and focused on the effort, not the outcome.

As a society, we tend to focus on the negative. A teacher marks in "red" the number wrong on a test, instead of marking the number correct in "green". If a child get 97 out of 100 correct, shouldn't the child be praised for the 97 and not discouraged over the three wrong? A coach tells a child how many errors they had on the baseball field. The coach doesn't highlight the number of runs, catches and throws made that were great, he simply focused on one or two errors.

Tips for Giving Practical Praise:

- Be specific. Don't tell your child "you are such a good baseball player," instead tell them what a great hit they had or what a great short-stop they are. Being specific is much better and helps children identify with a special skill.
- Say it when you mean it and be genuine. When you say "good job on that project," this tells children that you recognize the value of their hard work and efforts. It also tells them you know the difference between when they work hard at something and when it comes easy to them. Kids know when you are sincere. If you are not

sincere in your praise, children become insecure because they don't believe your positive words.

- Don't give praise where it isn't deserved. If your kids are constantly hearing how smart, handsome, pretty, bright, talented, or gifted they are it will begin to sound empty and have little meaning. Praise children for their effort and hard work, not their inherent talents.

- Encourage them to try new things. Always praise kids for trying new things, like riding a bike, a new food, or learning to tie shoes, and for not being afraid to make mistakes.

- Teach your children to take the "t" out of can't.

- Allow your children to overhear you talking about them in a positive way to others. They will believe you are more sincere.

Chapter Five

Negative Talk

"No one can make you feel inferior without your consent." -Eleanor Roosevelt

Hold Your Tongue

Things you DON'T say to a child:
- I hate you.
- I don't care.
- Leave me alone.
- Go away.
- Hurry.
- Give me a minute.
- Act your age.
- You're such a cry baby.
- Don't cry.
- You better stop or I'll give you a reason to cry.
- You are just like your (father, mother, sister, brother).

- I'm going to leave without you.
- Why can't you be more like your (sister, brother, cousin)?
- You aren't worth it.
- Don't you get it?
- Do it or else.
- You're so...
- You're bad.
- You know better than that.
- What's wrong with you?
- Wait until your (dad, mom) comes home.
- You shouldn't have missed that ball, pass, or goal.
- You shouldn't try out for sports. No one in our family was ever good at sports.
- You will never go to college. You aren't smart enough to go to college.
- You can't imagine the day I've had – when your child comes home from school and tries to ask you something.
- Great job! Or Good girl! – Every time they do something.

Chapter Six

Be a Good Role Model

"Example is not the main thing in influencing others. It is the only thing."-Albert Schweitzer

Kids Learn by Example

Kids are like sponges, they notice everything. Children have a tendency to model after those they are closest to first unless they make a conscious effort to break the mold. As parents, we should model the behavior and character we hope our children will have and continue to live by the rules that are set. Show them by example and verbal explanations.

You should:
- Pay attention to what you say or do around them and think about what kind of example you make.

- Teach your kids about charity. One example is to get involved and take your children to a local soup kitchen or homeless shelter and help serve meals. Explain to them why you do acts of charity so they understand why they should.
- Teach kids about chores by setting a schedule and having them help you. Don't tell your child to do something, but ask for their help. Take time to demonstrate first exactly what you want. The earlier children learn to help, the longer they will be willing to help.
- Listen to them. Utilize the active listening from Chapter 2 on Positive Parenting Behaviors.
- If you want your children to share, set a good example and share with them.
- Instill a sense of belonging by displaying their pictures and family pictures on the walls of the home.
- Avoid favoritism. Surveys show that most parents have favorites, but most children

believe they are the favorite. Always be fair and neutral.

- Teach your children about making the right life choices. Allow your kids to experience life for themselves by not making decisions and choices for them all the time. They must learn to live with the consequences from the choices they make. By doing so, it helps them to become good decision makers and problem solvers so that they are prepared for independence and adulthood.

- Reflect on your own childhood experiences. Identify mistakes you feel your parents may have made, and make every effort to avoid passing them on to the next several generations.

- Be the best role model you can by giving up your bad habits. Gambling, smoking, alcohol and drugs can jeopardize your child's future. These habits can create a number of health hazards (including cancer from second hand smoke) or a financial disaster for everyone. Alcohol and drugs can also introduce violence to your child's environment.

- Be careful not to strictly follow the parental behavioral stereotypes of your culture, race, ethnic group, family, or other defining factors. What may have worked for one generation may not work for another.

Conclusion

"We may not be able to prepare the future for our children, but we can at least prepare our children for the future." -Franklin D. Roosevelt

Being a parent is one of the best life experiences a person can have. One of the most important things a parent can give their child is to know they are loved. Tell them you love them every day. Give lots of hugs and kisses. Love them without conditions; don't force them to be who you think they should be in order for them to earn your love. Let them know that you will always love them no matter what. Encourage them to talk to you about everything with no consequences.

No matter what parenting style you choose, you will discover that you will adapt different parenting styles based on your children's personality. Don't be afraid to be a parent.

Parenting doesn't stop when a child becomes an adult. Being a good parent remains a life-long role. However, once they become adults, the decisions and choices they make in life are ultimately theirs along with the consequences.

Self-Discovery Challenge

List 3 things you will consider doing:

1._____

2. _____

3. _____

List 3 things you will implement today:

1._____

2. _____

3. _____

List 3 things you will no longer do:

1._____

2. _____

3. _____

List 5 things to teach your children about what parenting means:

1._____

2. _____

3. _____

4. _____

5. _____

About the Author

MICHELE SFAKIANOS is a wife, mother, and grandmother living in Fort Myers, Florida. In 1982, she received her associate in science degree in business data processing/computer programming. In 1993, she received her associate in science degree in nursing from St. Petersburg Junior College, graduating with honors. In 1999, Michele received her Bachelor of Science degree in nursing from Florida International University, graduating with high honors. In 2009, she received her real estate sales associate license. Michele has worked her way through the nursing areas, including medical/surgical, pediatrics, oncology, recruitment, and nursing informatics. Michele has been previously published in two poetry books and a nursing journal. She continues to be an award-winning author of: *The 4-1-1 on Life Skills; The 4-1-1 on Step Parenting; and The 4-1-1 on Surviving Teenhood*. She is well respected in her areas of expertise. Her years of experience as a registered nurse, mother, and leading authority on Life Skills and Parenting have given her the knowledge and wisdom to write her books.

Open Pages Publishing, LLC

Open Pages Publishing, LLC is a self-publishing company offering books to inspire, teach, and inform readers. We specialize in a variety of subjects including: life skills, self-help, reference, parenting, and teens.

Open Pages Publishing books are available at all major online book retailers. They may also be purchased for educational, business, or promotional use.

For bulk orders: special discounts are available on bulk orders. For details contact our sales staff at:

info@openpagespublishing.com.

If you would like to receive an autographed copy of this book or other books published by the author, please email the following information to:

info@openpagespublishing.com

- Full Name
- Address (street address, city, state, zip, country)
- Phone Number (including area code)
- Indicate which book(s) you are interested in:
    - The 4-1-1 on Life Skills
    - The 4-1-1 on Step Parenting
    - The 4-1-1 on Surviving Teenhood
    - Parenting with an Edge
    - Teen Success: It's All About You! Your Choices – Your Life
- Name of the person the autograph is for.
- Indicate if for a special occasion (birthday, anniversary, graduation).
- Payment methods include Visa, Master-Card, Discover, American Express, and PayPal.

20461897R00031

Printed in Great Britain
by Amazon